MW01130175

In Loving Memory of:

Cooper Danielle Jeans

ALWAYS IN MY PRAYERS, FOREVER IN MY HEART

BY
NATALIE JEANS

ILLUSTRATED BY
OMAR GUTIERREZ

I found out mommy and daddy were having another baby. I was excited about being a big brother!

Big Bro

They even let me pick the name for the baby. I liked Hunter for a boy and for a girl I chose Cooper.

I wanted a baby brother,
but a baby sister was fine too.

I was looking forward to all
of the fun things we were
going to do.

As mommy's belly grew bigger,
I knew the baby would come soon.
We went out to dinner one night
and mommy surprised daddy with
pink balloons.

I was going to have a baby sister
and I was as happy
as could be.

I called her MY baby and would rub and kiss mommy's belly.

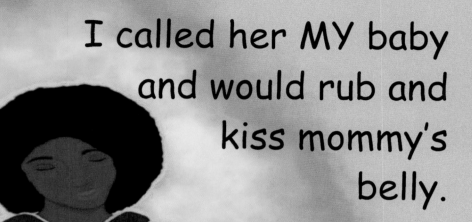

I always said, "Goodnight,
I love you Cooper" before
I went to bed.

And I included her in my prayers before resting my head.

So when mommy went to the hospital,
I was worried and afraid.

But I went on to school like a big boy,
I was so very brave.

I went to visit mommy in the hospital and she told me that my baby sister was sick.

I tried giving mommy a little apple juice,
"Here mommy drink this, it will help Cooper
feel better, that will do the trick".

The doctors tried all they could,
but Cooper did not get better
and could not go home that day.

God wanted her to come to Heaven
with Him, so she had to go away.

Heaven is a place where Cooper will no longer be sick. She will be there forever and cannot come back.

And though she is gone, she will never forget me. I'm still her big brother and that's a fact.

Mommy said it is normal to feel sad because losing a baby is a hard thing to go through.

Sometimes I feel angry because I did not get to hold her, mommy said that is ok too.

There are times I see mommy crying because she is sad that Cooper could not stay.

Sometimes people cry when someone that they love has to go away.

It is ok to miss my baby sister, mommy and daddy miss her too.

It is ok to still love my baby sister, mommy and daddy still do.

I know I cannot see my baby sister,
but these memories
I will hold onto.

She will forever be in my heart,
she is a part of everything
that I do.

Made in the USA
Coppell, TX
15 January 2020

14510904R00019